READY, C.

HOW TO FIND, ENTER AND WIN
ONLINE SWEEPSTAKES

(Enjoy this FREE profitable hobby and watch as
wins are delivered to your door)

By Sharon Elaine

Booklocker.com, Inc.
2007

Sharon has a web site with many areas of interest, including:

- Pictures of Sharon's wins

- Sharon's books and CDs

- Sharon's Bio, Blog and Newsletter

- Sign-up area to join Sharon's Affirmation Focus Groups

Sharon's web site is:

http://www.unleashedminds.com

I dedicate this book to everyone in my

wonderful family.

You all mean the world to me.

ACKNOWLEDGMENTS

I wish to give a special thanks to those in my life who support and love me. I don't know what I'd do without them, and I cherish and value them all.

My wonderful children, Becky, Justin and Nick are the lights of my life and I'm so honored to be their Earth mother.

My soul mate, Kevin, who loves me just as I am, and who is my rock.

My parents, June and Elmer, deserve many thanks for supporting me and believing in me throughout my life.

My sisters Debbie and Pam. I'm so honored to have them as my big sisters.

My fabulous cousin Felicia Oswalt, my sensational friend Sherri Harsh, Anita Hillin, Nathan Rankin (in spirit); Shannon…wherever you are; Kathy Hanson; Shari Hauck; Ken Adi-Ring, Joyce Slater; Iris Smithers, Tami Coyne; Helen Gray; Dottie Pendleton; Angel Hughes; Bob Schroeder; Bill and Shirley Schuhart; Dave and Stephanie Schuhart; Marilyn and Felix Childress, Neo and Nathan (our puppies); my students that I teach at Fox Valley Technical College and Lourdes High School; and all of the wonderful, amazing women on my Sweepstakes online discussion board.

Chapters:

CHAPTER ONE - Introduction of Sweepstakes

So, you want to win some online sweepstakes prizes? GOOD!   You came to the right place, and to the right person.

I started entering sweepstakes seriously in about 1998, even though I've won big items my whole life. I enter online sweepstakes every single day, unless I'm away on vacation (and then I really miss them).

It's a lucrative and enjoyable hobby, from finding the sweeps, entering them, and hearing that you've won, to finding the boxes of wins at your door.

There is a chapter with pictures and stories of my wins later in the book, to help keep you motivated. I'll also share stories of people who changed their "I never win anything" attitude, and soon began to win small items, and then a few more, now they are regular winners of sweepstakes prizes. And you can be too!

When I first started out, there wasn't much information about this hobby, nor was it even referred to as a hobby. The sweepstakes were also mainly entered with the method we now refer to as "snail mail" (regular postal mail). You had to spend a great deal of time on it, filling out papers and envelopes and spending money on postage. It was time-consuming, expensive (postage), and a bit annoying.

Now, most sweepstakes are entered online, for free, and with the tools I'll be sharing with you in this book, you'll be able to:

- Find the legitimate sweepstakes
- Enter them quickly (with software that fills in the form for you)
- Store the daily sweeps so you can enter them often
- Quickly delete the sweeps once they have expired
- Reap the rewards/prizes that come to your door

There will be radical thoughts in this book, like "be happy when others win", and "the more you believe you'll win, you'll win" and more. Take them or leave them, but you're reading a book by someone who has used those very ideas when approaching the sweepstakes hobby, and has benefited from them greatly.

I've included information about what to do once you win a big prize, how to fill out the required proof of identity and more.

It's also vitally important to avoid scams and rip-offs that are designed to look like legitimate sweepstakes. This book discusses many of the ways to uncover and avoid these scams, as well as how to keep your computer safe.

Well, enough chit-chat, let's get started! The sooner we get this information in motion, the quicker you become one of an ever-growing group of on-line sweepstakes winners.

Fun note:

(On this day... the day I'm sending the final version of this book to my publisher... I, swear to God, just won an all-expense-paid, all-inclusive trip to Cancun, Mexico, plus luggage and a $400 mixer. The trip is worth almost $4,000. Keep the faith and let's get you winning trips too!)

CHAPTER TWO – Rules of Thumb

I've won a lot of sweepstakes over the years. Some of them grand prizes, some not, but ALL very fun (and easy) to win.

I hear a lot of things from people when they hear about my sweepstakes wins.

Common Sweepstakes Myths:
- They aren't real, or if they are, only "other people" win them
- They're too hard to find
- They're usually scams
- They have too many people entering them, with crazy odds, so I could never win
- They're too much trouble to enter
- They have some kind of "catch" associated with them

One of my favorite conversations was with a woman who asked me:

"Don't you know the impossible odds of someone winning something like that?"   I smiled at her and answered "I guess not, I'm too busy winning the sweepstakes to check out those kinds of things."

RULE OF THUMB #1:

DON'T CHECK THE ODDS!

Any mental focus at all that makes you believe you may not win is not a good focus, and if you convince your mind that there is no "logical" way that you could win, you'll have lost the game before you even play it.

I don't have a logical explanation for why I win so many sweepstakes. I just enjoy winning them, and EXPECT to win them. One of the surest ways to NOT win a prize in a sweepstakes is to check the odds of winning. Just avoid that focus altogether.

RULE OF THUMB #2:

YOU go looking for the sweepstakes, don't let them come looking for you.

If you get an email (or worse yet, a flashing pop-up window online) which is urging you to enter it or "click here for your prize", immediately ignore them. Most of them are scams and are the surest way to get some kind of virus or spy-ware added to your computer.

There are THOUSANDS of legitimate sweepstakes, run by legitimate companies. It is your job to find them and to enter them (and to WIN them!)

Why do companies run these sweepstakes? For advertisement and marketing, of course. By sponsoring a sweepstakes, they are getting you to come to their website and focus on their name and product(s). I suspect there is a hefty tax deduction involved as well, though don't quote me on that.

When you enter sweeps frequently, you'll notice a few big companies that stand out as "regulars", and provide sweeps on a consistent basis. Many smaller companies are also reputable, but usually offer less expensive prizes. It will be up to you to decide if these lesser prizes are worth your time and effort to enter their sweepstakes.

With a smaller prize, I usually enter that sweep only once and then move on. It's usually not worth my time to add it to my list of daily's and keep entering it over and over again. But at least entering it once gets me "in the game" for that sweep, and I've won DVD movies and books from sweeps with my one entry picked as the winning entry.

RULE OF THUMB #3

Once you enter it, LET IT GO.

If you obsess over a sweepstakes and wonder:

- if winners have been chosen yet
- what the odds are
- how many times you've entered it
- if you'll win it
- if you'll be home when they call you
- if you have to sign for a package when they deliver it

...and in any way focus too much on any one or two sweeps, you lose the flow, joy and energy of the entire process. I enter a sweep, visualize myself winning the item for a bit, then I move on to the next.

I know of many people who keep charts and graphs of when they entered such-and-such sweep, and how many times they entered them, etc., etc. What a way to take the fun out of it all, in my opinion. Feel free to create a spreadsheet and do something like this if you like. I don't do this. If I win, great, if I don't, fine. There are always more sweeps coming along that I can win.

Keep your energy flowing and joyful or you'll stagnate and turn a fun hobby into a stressful job that you'll begin to resent.

RULE OF THUMB #4

Get your mind right!

"Whether you think you can, or you think you can't, either way you're right". Henry Ford

I'll add a quote of my own today:

If you believe you'll win, you will win, if you believe you won't win, you won't. Sharon Elaine

I can't tell you how many people hear of my wins and immediately state their own (negative) affirmation of "I never win anything".

It's not just the words that concern me; however, it's the BELIEF itself. You don't have to immediately begin to believe you will win every sweeps you enter, but you must be open to the idea of believing there is a good chance that you'll begin to win some of them.

Therefore...get your mind right. You must begin to at least introduce the idea and belief that you WILL win. If you go into this hobby of sweepstaking with the attitude of "I'll enter, but I probably won't win"... DON'T ENTER! It's a waste of your time. It won't be fun to enter, and you won't win.

NOTE: To further your positive mind-set, check out my book "The Book of Affirmations", by Sharon Elaine. It is also available through Booklocker, and on Amazon.com and bn.com. Using these positive affirmations daily will greatly increase your ability to pull wins to yourself.

RULE OF THUMB #5

Be patient.

At the beginning of sweepstaking, it understandably takes time to begin receiving prizes. Many times the sweeps have to end before they organize and mail out the wins.

All professional sweepstakers go through dry-spells when we scratch our heads and ask if it's worth it. But before long either the dam will break and lots of wins happen again, or a BIG win will occur, which makes it all worth it. BE PATIENT and keep entering, and STAY positive.

RULE OF THUMB #6

HAVE FUN!

Yes, there is a bit of work involved in the beginning, in learning how it's all done, and setting everything up and so forth, but don't let that scare you. Once you get past that, it should be FUN to enter your sweepstakes. For those of us who love entering sweeps, it's usually one of the lightest, most enjoyable parts of our day. It's something I always look forward to.

Note: Remember...if you need help with positive self-talk, you may wish to check out my book "The Book of Affirmations", which contains over 5,000 affirmations in many different categories. Check it out on my web site:

http://www.unleashedminds.com

CHAPTER THREE – The Basics

The basics – how to **FIND** sweepstakes, **ENTER** and **WIN**!

So what is involved in entering sweepstakes? Is it complicated? Is it dangerous? How many steps are really involved in entering online sweepstakes?

The word "Sweepstakes" confuses some people at first. They immediately think "lottery", which has them thinking "no way can I win that". Even though winning a sweepstakes is not a sure thing, it IS much more possible to win one of many sweepstakes prizes than, perhaps, winning a huge multi-state lottery.

This book is dedicated to information about ONLINE sweepstakes entry, as that is the direction most sweepstakes are now taking. Sure, there are still the occasional "snail mail" entries (regular postal mail), but they are getting more old-fashioned and I think will one day disappear altogether.

One reason, is that there is a great deal of work involved in entering these snail mail sweepstakes and people are getting more and more short of time these days. (Some people even think it takes too long to fill out ONLINE sweepstakes forms!)

The thing I never understood about snail mail sweeps is that they made them SO specific, and if you detoured from any of their strict requirements by even an INCH, you were disqualified. (Filling out a 4" by 5" card instead of a 3" x 5" card, for example), or forgetting to spell out your state completely instead of doing a 2-character abbreviation.

You had to enter them by hand, so it was time-consuming, a bit annoying, and the postage could add up quickly. *(It's far cheaper to buy this book and learn how to enter them FOR FREE than it is to buy postage for sweepstakes like the old days.)*

People are often suspicious about why companies give away these big prizes. However, increasing traffic to a company's web site is beneficial to that company in many ways. By attracting you to their web site, they're hoping you will find out more about their products and services and might even be compelled to buy a few things, or come back to their web site again later. Sweepstakes can be used as a powerful advertising tool.

Only a small percentage of people know about online sweepstakes. When they DO happen to hear about them, many think they're only scams and think you're stupid to even think about entering them. They shy away from them, and do not understand the truth of what they REALLY are.

You, on the other hand, were smart enough to get this book and find out about this ever-growing hobby, and will begin to benefit from the knowledge (and the prizes you'll win) all that much sooner.

Be sure to check out the **Sweepstakes Computer Safety** chapter to find information of how to keep you and your computer safe.

THE BASICS - LEVEL ONE
How to Find Legitimate Sweepstakes

There are many web sites dedicated to sharing information about legitimate sweepstakes. I will share a few of my favorites here.

My personal favorite, and the one I've gotten the most used to using, is Sweepstakes Advantage. The web site address is:

http://www.sweepsadvantage.com

Once you get to this web site, you may wander around finding the sweeps in any way that makes you comfortable.

If you're interested in how **I** do it, I always click on the "**new sweepstakes**" link. They have the sweepstakes laid out well... first, by the date the different sweeps were entered onto their web site, and then in categories such as:

24 Hour Entry
Daily
One Time Only
Unlimited
Weekly
Monthly
Instant Win
Odd Entry

(If you're wondering what the difference between 24 Hour Entry and Daily is… the 24-hour entry will only let you enter once within 24 hours. If you enter at 10 p.m. today, you won't be able to enter that sweeps until at least 10 p.m. tomorrow. Daily's start the day over at midnight or so, and you could perhaps enter the sweeps at 8 p.m. today and then again at 8 a.m. tomorrow, which is once per day, not specifically 24 hours.)

I will describe the steps I take in my sweepstakes ritual and then will suggest other web sites and ideas in case you'd like to collect yours in a different manner.

Sharon's Step One –

I click on the "**new sweepstakes**" link on the web site mentioned above, then click on the date. Each day's date is a link to the sweepstakes that they are sharing with everyone for that day.

Sharon's Step Two –

I read the prize information under a sweepstakes heading (to determine if I am eligible and if I want to enter it or not).

(Remember, you don't have to enter every sweepstakes that comes down the pike... guidelines for how to choose which sweepstakes are for YOU are included below as well)

Sharon's Step Three –

I then click on the link heading to access an individual sweepstakes.   It opens up a new window with that sweepstakes in it.

> *If it looks like something I'd like to continue to enter every day, until it expires, I then copy and paste it into a program I'll be talking about in Step 3 below (called "Sweeps").   The steps involved for how to Copy and Paste are also included below.*

I then enter that sweepstakes, using Roboform (the information in Level Two below), and then move onto the next sweepstakes in the list.

I do this for the 24 Hour Entry, the Daily's and the Instant Wins. For the One Time Only sweepstakes, I enter them... well... one time only and then move on. You can enter these only once, at any time until the sweeps expires.

Some people like One Time Only's more than the Daily's, as it gives everyone the same odds of winning, as everyone gets only ONE entry. I WILL say that the grand prizes I've received over the past few years; have come from these One Time Only sweeps.

(Note: For a list of many other Sweepstakes and Contest entry web sites and information, look at the end of this chapter below.)

THE BASICS - LEVEL TWO
Filling out the entry form, using Roboform

Ahhhh Roboform, marvelous Roboform... one of my favorite software products EVER! And the good news is... you can get a free copy of it to download to your computer. I WILL say that after you've been using it for a while and want to continue with it, you may consider purchasing it, as I eventually did. It's well worth the $30 or so that it costs.

Let's talk about how to get it, and what it does. You can find it at **http://www.roboform.com** There is a free download and another download where you buy it. Choose whichever you wish. It will begin to download. You may have to say "yes" or make a few choices along the way, but it is easy to let it download to your computer. It may or may not ask you to restart your computer to complete the installation process.

Note: If you use Mozilla Firefox as your browser, you'll need to download an additional adapter, which is free, and is also available as part of the Roboform installation.

So, what does Roboform do? It helps you to quickly fill in sweepstakes forms (and any other online form, such as when you are ordering products online).

Once you have downloaded Roboform, it allows you to fill in whichever fields of information that you wish to place within your personal profile.

Some examples of the fields of information that you will want to fill out and save in your profile, are:

First name
Last name
Address
City, State, Zip
Phone number
Fax number
Email address
Age
Sex

I do NOT recommend filling anything into your Roboform profile that has private information such as your social security number, credit cards, bank accounts, etc.

The area in which to fill out your profile information looks something like this:

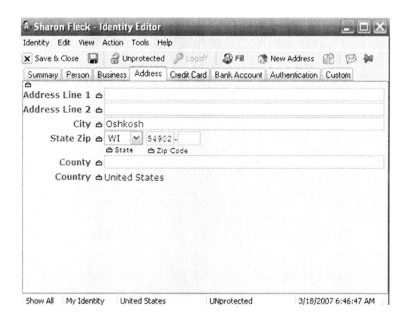

Filling out future forms then becomes a simple process. As soon as a form that needs to be filled in comes up on your screen, a small Roboform window pops up and basically asks "would you like us to fill out this form?"

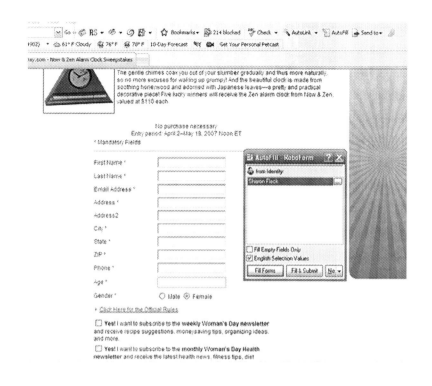

You click on "Fill form" (as seen in the example) and POOF! The fields are instantly filled in for you! See how much time that saves? Roboform enables me to enter over 200 sweepstakes every day, on my laptop computer, while I'm watching TV with my family.

Unfortunately it does not always fill all the forms in completely, or completely right, but it's not Roboform's fault. As a web site creator myself, I know that many people create their sites incorrectly (especially the field names in their forms), so you WILL need to proof your entry before you hit "submit" and make sure everything is filled out correctly to have a legitimate entry.

Roboform also allows you to save your sign-in or log-in information for various sweepstakes sites. If you are using the free version of the software, you are limited to how many username and password combinations you can save. When you purchase Roboform, it is unlimited.

It works out very well when you create a username/password for a sweepstakes, and want to enter that sweepstakes again every day. It takes literally seconds to enter a sweepstakes in which Roboform has recorded the sign-in information.

One of the things you'll need to make sure you have "checked" each time is some variation of: "I agree to the rules and regulations of this sweepstakes".

Should you take the time to read the rules? Well, that's up to you, but here are some good reasons to read the rules:

1. They tell you whether or not you are eligible
    - Are you within the age range required
    - Do you work for the sponsor company (makes you ineligible)
    - Do you live in a state (or country) that allows this sweepstakes
    - Can more than one from your household enter
    - If it is a trip, do you have what is required, such as a passport, days off work for the days the trip runs, etc.

2. They tell you how you will be notified when you are chosen as a winner and how to write or check online for a list of winners when the sweeps is over.

3. If it's a CONTEST (vs. a sweepstakes), they will tell you, in detail, what is required to enter. Contests require you to complete something like: providing a photo, or a recipe or a short essay or story and so forth.

Something else that comes up on many sweepstakes entry forms is a **Verification Code**.

This is a code (letters and numbers) embedded either in a picture or within wavy lines, etc., that you will need to duplicate/type-in within the field area they provide.

This is usually used to keep people from cheating by using "mass-entry" programs. These mass-entry types of programs are designed to enter you in hundreds and perhaps thousands of sweepstakes automatically, where you don't have to even visit the sweepstakes web site.

As you can imagine I'm VERY much against these types of cheating methods, therefore, I'm glad to see the Verification Codes on sweepstakes, as it lets me know they are doing all they can to avoid cheaters.

Many of the verification codes are not case sensitive, but some are, so if you get an error when putting them in, try to put them in exactly as shown.

THE BASICS - LEVEL THREE
Organizing your sweepstakes

Sure you could use the Favorites area in your browser, but it doesn't have a convenient way to store information about any entry codes you need to remember, or the sweepstakes ending date. It's irritating to take the time to enter a daily sweep, only to find out that you've been entering a sweep that closed three weeks earlier.

Here is a great (free) software you can download to organize your Sweeps (though, once again, I recommend giving the creator a donation)

You can find Sweep at

http://www.wavget.com/sweep.html
Download this free software to your computer.

With the current sweepstakes I have saved in mine, it looks like this:

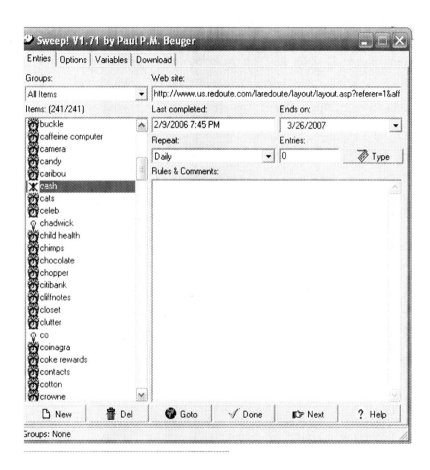

How to use Sweep software

When you find a sweepstakes that you would like to enter more than once, you will want to add that sweepstakes to your Sweep software.

Adding Sweepstakes to Sweep software:

1. Click on the "New" button on the bottom left.
2. Give it a name, any name you like (there can't be more than one item with the same name)
3. Copy and paste the web site address into the top line (instructions to copy and paste are below)
4. Choose the ending date from the drop-down calendar on the right side. (you'll find the ending date within the rules of the sweepstakes)
5. Choose whether it is a "daily" "weekly", etc.
6. Type information in the bigger, body section

Some items to put in this body section would be:

- Whether or not it's an instant win (on the days when I'm pressed for time, I check this area and ONLY enter the Instant Wins for that day)
- Information on how often to enter (for example, some let you enter multiple times a day)
- Information on who you're entering for (I enter for my young son on the sweeps where there is an age requirement that he fits)
- Any special codes that are required for entry
- Reminders to yourself of where to find the sweeps on the web page

Deleting Sweepstakes from Sweep software:

1. Left-click on the name of the sweep
2. Click on "del" (looks like a little trashcan)
3. When it asks you if you are sure, click on "yes"

That's all there is to it.

The nice thing about this software is that it puts a new icon (a yellow lantern) to the left of the sweepstakes name on the last day you can enter that sweep, and a big "X" over the icon on the day the sweeps is now expired. It makes it really easy for you to see when it's time to delete a sweepstakes from the list.

Using Sweep software:

It's simple to use this software to enter sweepstakes. You simply:

1. Double-left-click on the NAME of the sweepstakes, and it will open that web site.

That's it. Then you're ready to enter your information (with Roboform!).

Oh, there's one more thing... EXPECT to win something every day! It keeps your focus positive.

I always tell people "I'm off to win some sweepstakes", instead of "I'm off to enter some sweepstakes". It's another positive focus.

How to copy and paste:

Copying and pasting can be done anywhere on your computer, and the steps I'll be sharing here may help you to copy and paste in other areas, for they're basically the same steps.

For sweepstakes copy and paste:

1. Have the sweepstakes you want to enter opened in a browser.
2. Left-click once in the Address Bar to highlight the URL/web site address.
3. Right-click in the Address Bar to get a short-cut menu to appear.
4. Left-click on "copy"
5. Go to the Sweeps software and right-click in the web site address area (after you've named the sweepstakes by clicking on "new" within the Sweeps software)
6. Left-click on "paste"

Sweepstakes and Contest Websites and Newsletters

There are many web sites and online newsletters that are devoted to finding and listing Sweepstakes. I've given my favorite web site link above, yet everyone should find the web site(s) they prefer. Try each one out for a bit and decide for yourself which one(s) you enjoy.

(Note: all of these web sites were working at the time of this publication, how long they will continue to work is anyone's guess)

Free Sweepstakes Web Sites:

http://www.bestsweepstakes.com/

http://www.online-sweepstakes.com

http://www.geocities.com/sweepershomepage/

http://www.contestnewsletter.com/

http://www.contestalley.com

http://www.ragstoriches.com/

http://www.contesthound.com

http://www.quicksweeps.com/

http://www.cashnetsweeps.com/

http://www.grandmajam.com

Instant win only site:

http://www.myinstantwin.com/

Pay newsletters: (These give you a trial issue then require payment to continue).

http://www.onlinesweeps.com/

http://www.sweepsheet.com/

http://www.redhotsweeps.com

Which Sweepstakes should you enter?

Some sweepstakes "experts" say that you will never find time to enter all the sweepstakes there are to enter. My response to that is... who would want to?

I figure out whether it's worth it to me to enter each sweep, based on whether I would want to pay taxes on the item if it's a grand prize, and whether I even WANT the item.

Granted, if I win an item I don't really want, I can always sell it or give it to someone else who might want it, but sometimes it's just nice to let someone who really WANTS to win that item, win it (like when the prize is meeting some star who is an unknown to me but makes some young girl swoon).

It's up to you how much time you want to spend entering sweepstakes. If you find that you are spending too much time on this hobby, or that you're not enjoying the entering process, then by all means slow down your entering. However, you may find that you begin to crave the process, and enjoy entering almost as much as winning... well I did say ALMOST.

****

KEEP A LIST OF YOUR WINS!!!   This is something I always "meant to do" but never kept up with in the initial years of winning. I always figured "I'll remember what I won later". Um, yeah. (Like when you have a brilliant idea in the middle of the night and think you'll remember it when you wake up).   Your brain has interesting ideas sometimes about what to remember and not remember.

I began to keep a list within the past couple of years, and I'm so glad I did. I've also tried to remember as many past wins as I can, and yet I know I've forgotten many, and it's a shame, as I really enjoy looking over my list of wins (especially if I haven't won anything for a while).

I also now put some my wins on my web site (**http://www.unleashedminds.com**) . You may choose to do the same thing with your wins, on a site of your own. It's fun to share pictures and information about your wins with friends and family on a simple web site that anyone can get to easily.

Taking pictures of your wins doesn't require a digital camera, but it sure helps. Having a digital camera makes it easy to take pictures of your wins and upload them to your computer quickly and easily. You can then send them as attachments in emails to show your friends and family, and even upload them to a file transfer area for use on your web site.

I also take Screen Grabs/print-screen's of the instant win notifications, and digital pictures of the Congratulations notes and letters I receive. It's great to stay motivated about future wins, by looking at the growing collection of past wins.

I also keep a shelf (or two or three) in a closet for wins that I may not prefer to use myself. I keep them to give away to friends and family, especially at Christmas-time.   My family enjoys getting the free items so much; I keep the Congratulations note in with the item so they can see that it was a win. This past Christmas I had a record of 46 items on my Christmas present shelf of wins. It sure goes a long way in planning for Christmas, and makes it fun too.

CHAPTER FOUR – You've Won! Now What?

How you find out that you won

This chapter is about how you will be notified of your wins from the sponsor.

The FIRST is one of my favorites. It's when you go to get the mail, and on your way to the mailbox you spy a box... a pretty good-sized box... and then it dawns on you... you didn't order anything!

So you rush to the box, bring it in, and happen to notice in the upper-left hand corner of this box something like "Fullfillment Center", and your heart leaps into your throat.

IT'S A WIN!

Here's an example of what the winning message will say IN the box with the actual win. It's a bit fuzzy, but you can see the "congratulations" there I think.

Talk about the ultimate Surprise Box!

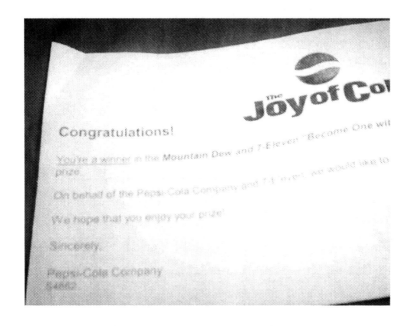

Many of these wonderful prize boxes have simply arrived at my door, without my previous knowledge of their coming. This one was an entire Xbox system, with extra Xbox speakers, and a game. It just arrived at the door while I happened to be talking to my Mom on the phone.

While on the phone, I heard the doorbell, so I gave my young son the phone to talk to his Nana while I got the door. I opened up the box and showed him what was inside. As he's an avid gamer, he became so excited that he immediately DROPPED THE PHONE to reach for the Xbox. I'll never forget that reaction.

Here is my son with that win.

These types of wins require nothing from you (except your original entry in the sweepstakes!). The sweepstakes has simply ended; they picked your name as one of the winners, and they sent the item to you. Poof, period, all done. FUN!

The SECOND way you can receive notification of your win is via email. These are sometimes the trickiest to trust, and I go into more detail about this in the Computer Safety chapter, so please check that out as well.

Here is an example of a real winning email notification.

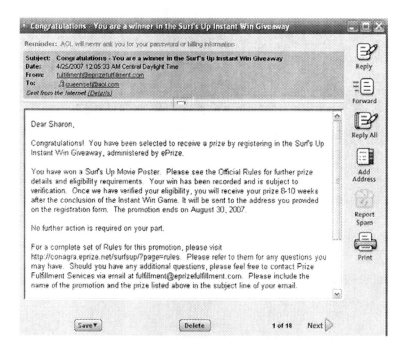

I save these emails to look at again when I haven't won for a while, to keep my spirits up until I win again.

Unfortunately some dishonest people have used fake "winning" emails to lure unsuspecting people to open up bogus emails and click on links within the email. Doing so often deposits spy-ware, ad-ware or viruses on their computers. Others use these fake congratulatory-type of emails in order to lure you to their gambling web sites.

Remain in control and trust yourself, and you will find it easier over time to discern what is and is not a legitimate win. (Remember that rule-of-thumb… "YOU go looking for sweepstakes, don't let them come looking for you, and DON'T send them any money!")

What's fun about email win notifications is how you can get excited when you receive the winning email notification AND again later when the win actually arrives.

That's also a fun ingredient in an Instant Win, which is our next type of notification.

This THIRD type of notification can be very exciting, though a bit confusing for some. It is the INSTANT notification, from playing what's called an INSTANT WIN SWEEPSTAKES.

These are legitimate sweepstakes; they simply allow you to instantly find out if you have won a prize. Here are a couple of example pictures.

Here's Kevin when we received that win.

There are lots of different ways instant wins are done, but the general guidelines are:

- Most (but not all) Instant Win sweepstakes are daily's, so you can play them once a day.

- Some (not all) of them require some kind of special code to get in (a product UPC code, as an example)

  In addition to finding it on the product itself, UPC codes can usually be found online on sweepstakes web sites.

- Once you have entered all the required information for the sweeps, there is oftentimes a game involved. It's usually very simple, and can be quite fun.

  There is one that lets you play three times a day and each time you shoot a basketball into a hoop. Others have racing games, and there are LOTS of games that look like a slot machine. You can play the game if you wish, but playing the game is NOT required to win the game.

I have a confession to make here. I do NOT usually play the games. Every once in a blue moon I'll click "spin" on one of the ones that looks like a slot machine.

What I do most-often, however, is I look for a link that says something like:

"Click here if you can't see the game"

I click on that right away, as it saves a lot of time (remember, I enter over 200 daily sweeps each day, and DO still want to have a life with my family).

> *Note: This is the way I enter all Instant wins, and I usually win at least one (usually more) a week, so you CAN win instant win games by doing what I do above.*

These instant win games are set up to have random wins at precise times during the day and night (as randomly chosen by the computer system). The next person who enters their entry on, or immediately after, the winning time will win the prize; therefore skill is not required to win.

Most times while you're busy staring and grinning at your winning notification screen, the company is busy sending you a confirmation email (see above about emails).

The same rules apply to what I wrote previously about emails. SOME of them will need you to respond and say that you DO want the item you won, but most of them will simply say something like "you do not need to do anything else, your prize will be sent to you in the next 6-8 weeks."

The FOURTH way you'll be notified of wins is, of course, by telephone.

It's smart to always be CAREFUL to avoid telephone scams, but you WILL need to answer your phone on a regular basis. FIVE of my big wins were told to me on the telephone, and these are just the ones I remember... there could have been more.

The first one was my win of a stair stepper, the second was my limo ride and VIP dinner at the dog track, the third was my television and bundle of movies and goodies, the fourth was the WWF tickets and meet-n-greet with the wrestlers, and the fifth was my $10,000 Thomasville furniture win.

On none of these calls did I have an overly-excited person on the other end of the line, acting fake or shifty and exclaiming how lucky I was that I won, or asking me for money or private information.

What you'll usually hear from a real telephone win notification is something like this:

You: hello?
Them: Hi, is (insert your name) available?
You: this is she, who is calling?
Them: Hi, this is Sandra from such-and-such company. DO YOU REMEMBER ENTERING the "Such-and-such Sweeptakes?"
You: I think so.
Them: Well, we are pleased to let you know that you are the POTENTIAL grand prize winner of this sweepstakes. The reason we say "potential" is that you'll need to prove you are who you say you are, and prove that you are eligible to win this prize.
You: What did I win? What did I win?
Them: Your potential grand prize is…. (insert prize) We will be sending you Affidavit of Eligibility via Federal Express and you will need to get it notarized and mail it back to us in the pre-paid envelope that we will also send to you. Here is my phone number, contact me with any questions.

****

This sample dialogue shows that they are real people, explaining your win in very easy terms. They do NOT sound overly fake or happy. They do not try to get you to buy something or send them money or give them information about yourself.

Anyone who calls you who does any of these red-flag things is probably NOT legitimate and, at best, I would ask a great deal of questions to feel comfortable before sending them any private information.

People ask me all the time whether you have to send them your Social Security Number, and are concerned that they have to do that for grand prizes. The problem is, if you DON'T give them this information IN YOUR AFFIDAVIT, NOT OVER THE PHONE, then they will not be able to award you your grand prize. They must send you a 1099 tax form at the end of the year, reflecting the total value of the prize, and you will be required to include the information from that 1099 form with your yearly taxes.

DON'T give out your social security number willy-nilly, or <u>anything</u> private like this over the phone, but you WILL be required to give it for any grand prize win when the value is higher.

This takes us full-circle, to being notified of your wins by mail, which would be the FIFTH of the notification methods. If you don't receive the prize by mail right away, you might receive notification of a prize some other way through the mail.

What I got recently was a letter from a sponsor, telling me I won a $100 spafinders gift certificate. The letter said that if my address was right, I didn't need to do anything, and the prize would be sent to me within a few weeks. They then gave me instructions for how to tell them if I had moved recently.

The mail is also useful for receiving the Affidavit's of Eligibility, which I spoke of earlier. These are only required when you win a larger prize and are usually sent to you via Federal Express, with a return Federal Express envelope within it, postage-paid.

If you receive information about a win (from any of the above methods) from a company other than the sponsor company, don't be overly concerned.

Many big companies who sponsor these sweepstakes use <u>prize distribution companies</u> who handle a great portion of the work of their sweepstakes. They accept the entries, randomly computer pick the winners, contact the winners, handle the affidavits of eligibility, and schedule the mailing of the winning items.

CHAPTER FIVE – Stories of My Wins

MY WINS
(The "NOTHING BUT FUN AND BRAGGIN'" chapter)

This chapter is here for a couple of important reasons:

1)   It's great for motivation. If I haven't won for a while, I like to look back at pictures and screen grabs of what I've already won. It keeps me going through the dry spells (and for most people, there ARE dry spells).

       I'm a REAL person, who has entered sweeps, the REGULAR online way, and I've won REAL prizes. So, feel free to check out this chapter for some motivation if you haven't won for a while.

2)   It's fun to brag ☺

THE STORIES:

My first really big win came along as quite a fluke. I got a phone call from a gentleman who told me I was the 5,000,000 prescription filled at ShopKo and that I won a stair-stepper machine (worth about $300 at the time).

Quite amazing, I felt, as I didn't have to fill out any forms or anything to win that one. I just had to have my prescription filled...and be lucky.

They asked me to come in and get my picture taken, which I did. I jokingly told my family that I hoped they didn't write next to my picture what my prescription was for. I could just see the sign saying something like: "Here is our winner. By having an anti-fungal prescription filled, she has won our grand prize"... Yikes!

That win led to many others, like my first win from a radio station. I happened to be listening to the radio one day while getting ready for work. I heard the announcer say:

"So, here's how this contest works... Every time you hear this sound..." (then he played the sound of a

greyhound bus) "...call in and if you're the first caller you get into the drawing for a limo ride and V.I.P. treatment and dinner for four at the greyhound race track".

I called in immediately as a joke, and said "I know you were explaining the rules, but did THAT time count? Cause I mean I DID hear the sound..." (...fully expecting him to say "no, smart-ass, call later") But he laughed and said "It sure DOES count, great job there!" I won a very small prize and been placed into the bin to potentially win the grand prize. I promptly forgot all about it.

Three weeks later, I got the phone call that my name was pulled amongst all the qualifying entries and I and three other friends went on a GREAT night at the race track. We were taken there in a limo, free dinner and drinks in an exclusive box with a TV in it, and much more V.I.P. treatment. We had the time of our lives.

Another fun tidbit about that night is that the radio station also gave away several wins of $108 in cash, throughout the evening, as they were sponsoring that night at the race track. They pulled my name AGAIN out of the 8,000 people who were at the race track that night. What are the ODDS of that? (Once again, NOT believing in odds has served me very well).

Another couple of big wins came about through the job I had about 15 years ago, as a computer instructor. I had already thoroughly convinced my co-worker and best friend that I win things easily (she was one of the four in the limo trip, above). So, when we sat down at a business meeting one day, and found out that someone in our company would be randomly picked to win a free trip to a seminar, we both grinned at one another and I winked at her. She said aloud "Well we know Sharon will win..." and I did.

At this same seminar there were several thousand participants, yet only four prizes to be given out at the end of the conference. I won TWO of the four prizes. One was a Porcelain Whale statue, and the other prize was a laptop computer (which back then weighed a ton).

I know my winning attitude has rubbed off on my children. When my daughter was about five years old she entered a coloring contest at a local restaurant. As we were leaving she turned in her entry and asked them, point-blank "When will you call to tell me that I won?" Sure enough, the next day, she got that winning call.

She's 22 now, and is here with a couple of recent wins (that showed up at my door)

Her twin brother then quickly won another contest. We were walking through the mall and noticed they had a local orchestra there.

They asked all the young children in the mall to come up and try to win a prize for "conducting" the musical group. My son put his heart and soul into his conducting, and won by a landslide, winning a huge backpack filled with school supplies.

This same son above (also 22 now... yes they are twins) was the one who answered the phone for my first big television win. He used to be the original skeptic, and now tells all of his friends that his Mom wins everything.

My youngest son recently won Guitar Hero II (a video game with a plastic guitar) by putting his name and $1 into a drawing at a local store.

The man there, who knew him from coming in so often to buy games, said "You'll never win with just one entry; some people have 20 or more entries in there". Nevertheless, my son got that winning call and here is a picture below of him with his first big win.

Another fun example of how important it is to **believe** that you will win comes from this same son. As long as we can remember, he has always won toy items from those claw machines. He's always just KNOWN he would win from them. When he was younger, he even likened it to candy machines, asking "Don't you just put the money in and the prize comes out? Like a candy machine?" (Don't you love it?)

Sure enough, even at the ripe old age of 14 now, he still gets wins every time he goes to claw machines. And I'm not talking about playing for hours. I'm talking about only a few quarters. Here is a picture of him the last time he won. In FOUR plays, he won FIVE prizes (two fell out at once on one attempt). Notice he's holding up 2 fingers, to show it's his 2nd big haul of wins. He's on a roll and taking after his Ma.

So what do you think? Think it pays to believe and KNOW you'll win? I sure think so, and so do all of my kids who have benefited from believing the same.

Even my fiancé has adopted this belief system. While at a local home show, I was putting my name into the bowls for wins, knowing I'd win something (I won a big, fluffy beach towel at that particular one).

Kevin put his name in to win an autographed baseball from Hank Aaron. As he handed in his entry form, he said "It's mine". And guess what? It was, and is. He has it proudly displayed on the bookshelf. Since then he has won several items in on-line sweepstakes as well, like a free movie ticket, several music downloads, and a $50 credit card.

One of my favorite winning moments was when I won the $10,000 worth of Thomasville furniture. Kevin was asleep when I got the notification that I won. I know how hard it is for him to wake up (we have that in common), so I waited a good 15 minutes or more after he woke up before I told him.

In the hallway, while wiping the sleep out of his eyes, he asked "So, have you had a good day so far today?" (Kinda bored-acting) Real nonchalantly I say "Yeah, I won something." After all, I tell him I win things all the time, as you'll see from the partial list of wins at the end of this chapter.

So I waited for him to peek into the room and say "Oh really, what did you win?" I gave him a silly grin and said "Oh, just $10,000 of Thomasville furniture..." and the look on his face is something I'll never forget. It was a combination of shock, joy, disbelief and more.

It's those kinds of looks and feelings that I concentrate on for future wins.

For a complete listing of my wins, and pictures of most of them, see them at my web site:

http://www.unleashedminds.com

CHAPTER SIX – Computer Safety

SWEEPSTAKES COMPUTER SAFETY

This chapter explains how to keep your computer optimized and SAFE while entering and winning sweepstakes.

I'm a computer instructor and have been working with computers since the age of 17 (I'm 47 now). I don't know EVERYTHING there is to know about computers, but I do know a few things to keep your computer safe and working optimally during your sweepstaking.

ADVICE NUMBER ONE:

One of the main bits of advice I always give, is to create an email address specifically for entering sweepstakes. This will keep your "spam" (unsolicited email) to a minimum within your regular email inbox. It will also allow you to check your emails a bit more carefully within this other sweepstakes mail account.

If you're unsure how to create a new email account, there are many places online which allow you to create free email accounts. **Hotmail.com** or **Yahoo.com** are two examples. After you have created your new email account, you can access this email from any computer that has internet access. You simply go to hotmail.com or yahoo.com and log into your email account.

When you fill out your forms to win sweepstakes, remember to put THIS special email address in when they ask you for an email.

Then, go and check this email several times a week, or preferably daily. Weed out any emails you don't want and delete them without opening them (these are the unsolicited emails you'll receive from visiting some of the sweepstakes sponsor sites).

Also, of course, it's important to check and see if you have any WINNING email notifications within this inbox. It is difficult to specifically show you what every legitimate winning email notification looks like, but I'll give you a few guidelines below.

1. It will have a return address that is something like fullfillmentcenter@___.com   MOST of the winning email notifications I've received have had something like this as the sender.

2. It will also have something like "October Dream Time Sweepstakes winner notification" in the subject line. Anything that is TOO exuberant or has the word "CONGRATULATIONS" a million times, is probably not legitimate.

3. Real notifications usually don't come with any HTML code (pictures) in the email. It is very simple and direct and has your confirmation and verification codes within it (and often-times the time and date that you played and won the sweeps).

4. Many real winning emails have an attachment of the RULES of the sweepstakes, in Word format, so you can read about your prize and the odds of winning, etc.

   Note: ALWAYS check the downloaded file with your virus-checking software before you open it into a program, to make sure it's virus-free! You can do this by downloading the file to your Desktop, then right-clicking on the file icon and choosing "check for viruses".

5. NEVER SEND MONEY OR CLICK ON ANY LINKS! Legitimate winning emails will never have you CLICK on anything. Even if you win a grand prize and they ask you to send in your Affidavit of Eligibility, they will send that in regular mail for you to fill out. You will not need to send money or click on anything within the email. Most winner notifications are pleasant and happy for you, but are also direct, to the point, and professional (and have no typing errors!)

6. They usually have their web site address within the body of the email, so you can copy and paste the web site address into your browser, to go to the web site and see if it looks familiar (like something you have entered previously).

7. You WILL find times when they ask you to hit "reply" if your information is correct, or to email them at a different email if you need to change your mailing address, etc.

8. DO NOT CLICK ON ANYTHING within any email that you don't know.

Therefore, create an email account specifically for sweepstakes and check it frequently.

ADVICE NUMBER TWO:

One thing my friends constantly hear me say regarding sweeps is...

"Go find the sweeps yourself, do NOT let them come looking for you".

This may seem unfair to those sponsors who send out legitimate emails or links with information about their most recent sweepstakes. It's true that you may have some legitimate companies looking for you to give you their sweepstakes information. However, a huge portion of the time, any time you see a blinking pop-up window or any other banner ad which is begging you to click on it, IT'S A SCAM or AD.

Remember, there are MANY legitimate web sites which will provide you with information on how to acquire sweepstakes. You don't want to risk the health of your computer by clicking on any ads that may or may not be above-board.

Check out the Basics Chapter of this book for complete information on how to find these sweepstakes web sites.

ADVICE NUMBER THREE:

There are several programs I recommend downloading and using (they are all free), which will help you delete unnecessary files and keep your computer running optimally.

The first software has a funny name, yet is does a great job. It is called Crap Cleaner, and can be found at: **http://www.ccleaner.com**

Once you download this program, run it on a regular basis (at least once a week) to remove things like: Temporary Internet Files, Cookies, Temp Files and more.

When entering sweepstakes, your computer will often get what are called "cookies" and other files in a folder called "Temporary Internet Files". These make your computer run slower over time, so it's best to keep them cleaned out on a regular basis.

There is a picture of what the software looks like below. It's easy to run. Once you've downloaded it to your computer, it will create an icon on your computer desktop. When you're ready to run it, simply double-left-click on the icon, to get basically what you see in the picture below.

The items that have checkmarks by them are the recommended areas of your computer where they will remove files. If you wish to uncheck any of them, you may, but I usually leave them all checked.

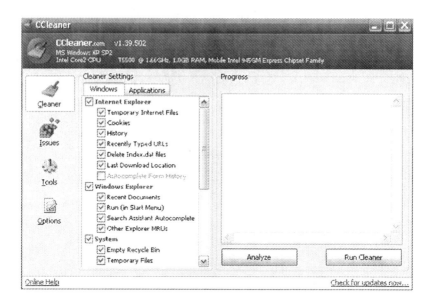

Then simply click on the button named "Run Cleaner" and it will run. It takes only a short time (less than a minute), and you'll be able to see how many files it has removed, and how much computer space you've gained.

The second software is called "A-squared" can be found at

http://www.emsisoft.com/en/software/free/

Downloading and running their free software searches for and removes small malicious programs that may have been secretly installed on your computer while you were on a sweeptakes or other web site.

As with the software above, once you download it to your computer, it will create an icon on your computer desktop.

When it's time to run it, I recommend adding an additional step, however. With these types of programs, they're only as good as how up-to-date your version of their software is, which means you'll need to check for "update now" (as you see in the picture on the next page).

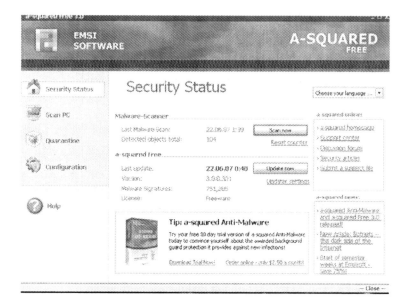

If there are updates to download, they are free, only take a few moments, and are HIGHLY recommended. Once you are up-to-date, it's time to click on the "Scan Now" button and allow this program to do its job.

I also recommend going to: http://**www.spybot.com** to download their free software to use for the same reasons. They both look for basically the same type of files, and yet one will find what the other doesn't.

(The "Tools" area of this program also has an excellent way to remove extraneous Start-up files from your computer, which allows you to have a quicker, more efficient computer experience.)

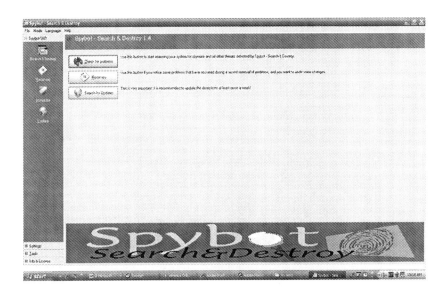

All of these software products, once installed, will place an icon (picture) on the background of your computer screen so you can find and use it easily. Simply double-click on the item, and choose to start the program.

You can continue working in other programs while they do their searching. When done, they show you what files they suggest removing. With a click of the mouse, the files are removed and you are once again safe.

The types of files these programs are looking for can do many things, from something as benign (though annoying) as recording where you go on the internet, to as spying and malicious as recording your keystrokes and passwords. They slow down your computer response time, and can cause security problems. They should be removed on a regular basis. I usually run these programs AT LEAST once a week, usually twice or more a week.

I run them in the order they are listed here. First I run Crap Cleaner, then A-squared, then Spybot. I then reboot my computer and am set for more sweepstakes entering!

NOTE: Everyone has spyware and adware on their computers, NOT just people who enter sweepstakes. Everyone should run these programs or others like them to keep their computer safe and running optimally.

ADVICE NUMBER FOUR:

Of course it's no surprise that I'll now be advising you to run your Virus-checking software on a regular basis. Simply put, viruses are small programs that, when opened and activated, cause intentional harm to your computer. They can be as simple as having your screen blink at you, or force you to continually reboot your computer, to as dangerous as erasing your hard drive information.

If you don't have Virus-checking software on your computer, there is a great, free one called **AVG** that can be found for a free download at

http://free.grisoft.com/doc/1

AVG is made by the same programmers who make the great browser **Mozilla Firefox**.

If you have not yet switched to **Mozilla Firefox** for your browser, you may wish to check into it. It helps to keep pop-up windows, spyware and other problems from attaching themselves to your computer.

If the above sites are no longer working when you read this, simply search for AVG (and/or Mozilla Firefox) on a search engine of your choice. You also can find both of these (and most downloads) at:

http://www.download.com

AVG is set up to automatically check for newer versions of their program every time your computer boots up. They download their new version, for free, to keep you up-to-date. As new viruses are created every day, it's important to keep this software as up-to-date as possible to keep your computer safe from them.

My AVG is set up to run a complete virus scan every morning at 8:00 a.m. You can set this up for yourself, when you first download their software. Set it up for a time when you will have your computer **on**, but at a time when it won't interfere with any important work, as it does slow system performance down a bit, temporarily, while it runs.

ADVICE NUMBER FIVE:

I spoke earlier of not letting sweepstakes "find you", but I want to elaborate on that a bit in this area, as there are many ways they can try to persuade you to go where you don't really want to go.

One way is by the use of the dreaded "Pop-ups". These are windows, usually smaller than a normal-sized program window, which seemingly spring out of nowhere (hence the name "pop-up") and set itself on top of your current open window.

There are also things called "Pop-unders" which pop-up on your screen and then seemingly disappear, but are really attaching themselves to your Task Bar (the big bar across the bottom of your screen). These aren't quite as annoying as the pop-ups, but they're a pain too.

Both of these are ways for an online advertiser to try to get your attention. They are hoping you'll click on the pop-up window (which is one huge link), and be taken to their web site.

If you DO fall for these, don't worry, just navigate back to the page you were working on, but do try to use a pop-up blocker (either within Mozilla, or one of your own through another program). Pop-ups slow down your sweepstakes entering as well, as you're constantly having to close out of these annoying things.

When you're on a web site, and you see a big ad that is blinking "You're our 999,999 visitor, click here to claim your prize of a new notebook computer". Try your best to just ignore it and scroll past it. Because, I hate to tell you, you're NOT their 999,999 visitor and if they do give you a new notebook computer, you're guaranteed to have lots of strings attached to it (and purchases needing to be made).

In general, be careful, but not paranoid. I wouldn't want to enter sweepstakes any more if they weren't fun, so I don't stay in a state of worry or fear when online. I just stay informed, and take the extra time to run the programs that keep me and my computer safe and efficient. I hope you will too.

CHAPTER SEVEN – Question and Answer

This chapter will explain a few fundamental terms and rules of sweepstakes, contests, freebies and surveys. While I don't know every rule of every giveaway, I will at least share a few bits of knowledge I've accumulated over the years.

Question: What is the difference between a Sweepstakes and a Contest?

Answer: Most sweepstakes require nothing from you except your information and perhaps a code. Some sweepstakes (sometimes called "contests") ask something from you. It could be something such as:

A photo
A short or long essay on the subject they choose
A recipe

In all instances, read the rules to determine what, if anything, you need to provide to enter the sweep.

Question: What are the limitations to sweepstakes; can I enter all of them?

Answer: Each web site that has information about sweepstakes and contests will include the limitations of each. Here are some examples of common limitations or exclusions:

Must be over 21 and a smoker to participate
Must be over 21 and have a valid driver's license
Must be between the ages of 13-24
Must be under 14
Must be over 18 and live in the US or Canada
Must be over 18 and live in Australia
Must own your own company to participate

There will be information about who CAN enter, and who can't. It's important to glance at this area first, before deciding whether you wish to enter a sweep, to make sure that you qualify.

Question: Do I have to read the entire rules page before I enter?

Answer: You don't have to, but it's a good idea to look for some basic rules, such as:

- What age you have to be
- How often you can enter

- If more than one person from your household is eligible to enter
- To see if you work for a company that they ban from entering the sweeps (for example if you work for Kraft, and they are the ones having this particular sweepstakes, they will usually prohibit Kraft employees and their families from entering)

Question: How do I find out if I won and if it's real?

Answer: This is a big subject, and a chapter is devoted to this. Also read the chapter about how to avoid scams.

Question: How do I copy a web site address into my Favorites or the Sweeps program?

Answer: Follow the next 7 steps:

- Get yourself to the web site that you wish to copy and save
- Left-click once in the web site Address bar... It should highlight/select the entire web address in preparation for the next step.

- RIGHT-click directly on the highlighted information and you should see a little gray menu appear.
- Left-click on "copy"
- Move yourself to where you want to save this information, like the Sweeps program.
- When you find the area where you wish to paste this web site address, RIGHT-click in the area
- Left-click on Paste

If you are not using the Sweeps program and prefer to save your daily sweeps into your Favorites (or Bookmark area), simply click on the button within your browser which lets you save it for future use.

Question: What do I do when I've won a big win, like a grand prize?

Answer:

1. Don't panic. You'll get through this.
2. Scream, jump around and be very, very happy and excited.
3. Check to see if there is anything else you need to do, like respond to the notification email with your correct address, or fill out an

affidavit of eligibility (proving you are who you say you are)

4. Follow the rules required, while constantly remembering to feel your gut for whether it is legitimate or not.
5. Ask any questions which come to mind. They will understand that you want to make sure that your win is legitimate and that you are excited and want to know all the details.
6. Do NOT send money. If you must pay taxes on this item, you will be sent the required paperwork at tax time.
7. Jump up and down with joy again, and tell everyone you know. I can't emphasize or recommend this step strongly enough.

ONE BIG SUGGESTION: If you take nothing else from this chapter, please take this information with you.   Check out prize details carefully BEFORE you enter a sweepstakes.

I'll give you an example of why I recommend this. A friend of mine won a purse that a sweepstakes indicated was worth $1,200. Because it was worth so much money, she had to pay taxes on it. She didn't really want the purse, but felt she could sell it. Turns out, she could NOT sell that purse, not even for $200 on Ebay. Yet she had to pay the taxes, and never carries the purse. That has to land somewhere in the "Top 10 Icky-feeling Wins List".

Another red flag for me is when the item seems way overvalued. For example, a "tricked-out" truck or motorcycle has a higher value due to the labor costs and "extras" that were put on the vehicle. However, you may or may not find the right market to sell this vehicle for its full estimated value.

I never enter a sweepstakes where I'm not wiling to pay the taxes. For instance, when entering for my $10,000 Thomasville furniture win, I had to ask myself if it was worth it to me, as I know I'd have a hefty chunk of taxes on that one.

Getting a full room of gorgeous furniture, INCLUDING king-sized mattresses, definitely made it worth it for me. It was a great decision as I enjoy my huge bed and beautiful bedroom set every day.

Pay close attention before you enter, and ask yourself these questions, so you don't get stuck with something you resent having won and can truly enjoy your wins long into the future. You want to be able to look at your win with total joy, and no bad memories attached to it.

Question: Can you make your own sweepstakes, and what is required?

Yes you can make your own sweepstakes, and the rules are pretty simple, as long as you don't make your sweepstakes requirements too limited.   In other words, if you choose to only let a certain age group enter, you will need to check into the legalities of that more carefully. There is a web site in the Basics chapter that may be able to help your further.

I have done a couple of different types of giveaways (which is truly what they are).

One of mine involved using Bravenet.com to create a form to put on my web site. The prize I offered was a free channeled reading. The form allowed me to let people enter the information I wanted to have. I then contacted a few of the main (free) sweepstakes sites, told them the rules I wanted to apply to the sweepstakes (that they could enter once monthly, for example), and gave them my information.

The next step was mine, where I put the link to the sweepstakes on my web site, so people who came to my web site could enter the sweep there.

When the month was up, I randomly chose the winner(s), then contacted them via email.

I also create sweepstakes each month on my online discussion board. The prizes depend upon which items I won the previous month that I didn't want. The people on the board are all fun and enjoy this small, unique sweepstakes.

I take digital camera pictures of each prize and then put that into the sweepstakes.

I usually then make it a random win, by asking each participant to give me a 4-digit number. I also give them an ending date and any other rules (like "may only enter once a day", etc.)

When the sweepstakes expires, I take all the numbers and match them against the pre-chosen number for each prize. The one who has guessed the closest to the number is the winner. I have them EMAIL me with their address (privacy is appreciated by all) and I mail out their win(s).

My dream is to win enough money to run my own big cash sweepstakes! I'd LOVE to hear of more of you starting your own sweepstakes, so we can all add something to the sweepstakes community!

Question: When filling out the entry forms does Roboform do it all?

Answer: Roboform, though a great program, does not always fill in all of the fields (or any of them, depending upon how the form is designed). You will always have to check over the form to make sure it's filled in correctly, and type in whatever is still needed.

Question: How long does it take to get my win?

Answer: Of course this depends entirely upon the rules of the sweepstakes. The rules may tell you approximately when they will begin to send out prizes, however, even THIS is not always accurate. For instance, I recently won $100, and it stated in the rules that they would begin to send out these

checks 6-8 weeks AFTER THE SWEEPSTAKES
ENDED (which would have been at least 8 months
from the date that I won) What happened instead,
is that I received the check within about 4 weeks
OF THE WIN.

Question: So what happens if you make an error
when you enter a sweep?

Answer: I have several examples of real friends
who have had troubles either entering sweeps, or
receiving their prizes.

One friend was entering a phone-in sweepstakes
trying to also win a rolling Gatorade cooler that I
had won the day before. Every day the recorded
voice on the other end had been saying "I'm sorry,
you didn't win today...". THIS day he said
"CONGRATULATIONS, stay on the phone so we can
get your address to send your rolling cooler".

Well, she got so excited, she was beside herself.
She stayed on the phone, quickly gave her
information and hung up and was so thrilled, until
her husband, who had been listening close-by, said
"You just gave them our name and street address;

you didn't give them our city or state". She was beside herself again... but this time with worry.

She called the company, and found the right person to talk to, and a month later, she got her cooler.

Sponsors WANT the legitimate winners to receive their prizes, and will work to make that happen.

That's why it's important to be able to PROVE that you are a legitimate winner. Screen grabs (print screens), email notifications and such are good ways to help you plead your case, if necessary. (For me, it's never been necessary.)

Most times, when you win an Instant Win, you'll be told to watch your inbox, as you will be receiving an email regarding the specifics of your win. Sometimes this email comes, and sometimes it doesn't. Your prize, however, almost always comes. I've only had ONE small prize, in all the years I've been doing sweeps, that didn't show up.

However, if you do not receive an email and are concerned that your instant win prize may not come (especially if it's a bigger prize), there is usually a contact person listed in the "rules" area of the sweeps information.

Unfortunately, there are people who try to get away with this when they have NOT won, and they're the ones who make it bad for the rest of us (honest) folks, so it's not uncommon to have to be very specific with your details in order to prove that you did, indeed, win.

Question: How do you do a Screen Grab or Print Screen?

Answer: This one is very simple, yet tremendously useful.

   a. Have your instant win showing on your screen
   b. Find the Prnt Scrn button on your keyboard (no, that's not a typo, that's usually how Print Screen is abbreviated on one of your keyboard buttons)
   c. Press this Prnt Scrn button
   d. If you want to put it in a program like Word, just go to that program, Right-click and choose "paste".

e. If you want to put it in a program like Photoshop, open up the program and choose "File", then "new".
f. Then click on "Edit", then "paste".
g. Then save the document (or picture) with a name you'll remember, so you can look at it again later.

Question: How do I become a part of your online discussion board, as I notice I need a password?

Answer: I chose to make it password protected due to some problems we had in the beginning when anyone and everyone could get in. Email me at: queensef@aol.com and I'll send you the password so you can join us.

Parting words

Thanks for joining with me in this book, and I hope you'll visit my web site at:
http://www.unleashedminds.com

I'd love to hear of your wins.

Happy Winning!

Printed in the United States
116584LV00003B/167/A

9 781601 453402